HAL•LEONARD

INSTRUMENTAL
PLAY-ALONG

AUDIO
ACCESS
INCLUDED

PLAYBACK+
Speed • Pitch • Balance • Loop

CLARINET

SUPERHERO THEMES

T0086841

Audio arrangements by Peter Deneff

To access audio, visit:
www.halleonard.com/mylibrary
Enter Code
5119-7732-3849-0462

ISBN 978-1-70513-159-6

Visit Hal Leonard Online at
www.halleonard.com

Contact us:
Hal Leonard
7777 West Bluemound Road
Milwaukee, WI 53213
Email: info@halleonard.com

In Europe, contact:
Hal Leonard Europe Limited
42 Wigmore Street
Marylebone, London, W1U 2RN
Email: info@halleonardeurope.com

In Australia, contact:
Hal Leonard Australia Pty. Ltd.
4 Lentara Court
Cheltenham, Victoria, 3192 Australia
Email: info@halleonard.com.au

THEME FROM ANT-MAN
from MARVEL'S ANT-MAN

CLARINET

Music by CHRISTOPHE BECK

WAKANDA
from BLACK PANTHER

Music by LUDWIG GÖRANSSON

THE AVENGERS

from THE AVENGERS

Clarinet

Composed by
ALAN SILVESTRI

BATMAN THEME

CLARINET

Words and Music by
NEAL HEFTI

CAPTAIN AMERICA MARCH

from CAPTAIN AMERICA

CLARINET

By ALAN SILVESTRI

ELASTIGIRL IS BACK
from INCREDIBLES 2

Clarinet

Composed by
MICHAEL GIACCHINO

IMMORTALS

from BIG HERO 6

Clarinet

Words and Music by ANDREW HURLEY,
JOE TROHMAN, PATRICK STUMP
and PETE WENTZ

GUARDIANS INFERNO

from GUARDIANS OF THE GALAXY VOL. 2

Clarinet

Words and Music by JAMES GUNN
and TYLER BATES

THE INCREDITS
from THE INCREDIBLES

Clarinet

Music by MICHAEL GIACCHINO

POW! POW! POW! - MR. INCREDIBLES THEME

from INCREDIBLES 2

Clarinet

Music and Lyrics by
MICHAEL GIACCHINO

IRON MAN
from IRON MAN

CLARINET

By RAMIN DJAWADI

ROCKETEER END TITLES

from THE ROCKETEER

Clarinet

By JAMES HORNER

THEME FROM SPIDER MAN

Clarinet

Written by BOB HARRIS
and PAUL FRANCIS WEBSTER

X-MEN: APOCALYPSE - END TITLES

from X-MEN: APOCALYPSE

CLARINET

By JOHN OTTMAN